Russia

Japan

Egypt

Nepal

China

India

Tanzania

For my daughter Zoë, the first to sit on my knee and share
the wonder of stories. Thank you for your encouragement
and support. I love you with all my heart.
Mum x

First published in the United Kingdom in 2020 by Lantana Publishing Ltd., London.
www.lantanapublishing.com

American edition published in 2020 by Lantana Publishing Ltd., UK.
info@lantanapublishing.com

Text & Illustration © Jo Loring-Fisher, 2020

The moral rights of the author-illustrator have been asserted.

Distributed in the United States and Canada by Lerner Publishing Group, Inc.
241 First Avenue North, Minneapolis, MN 55401 U.S.A.
For reading levels and more information, look for this title at www.lernerbooks.com
Cataloging-in-Publication Data Available.

Printed and bound in China.
Original artwork using mixed media, finished digitally.

ISBN: 978-1-911373-08-7
ISBN: 978-1-911373-36-0 eBook

Taking Time

Jo Loring-Fisher

LANTANA PUBLISHING

Taking time to listen to
a bird's song on the breeze.

Taking time to gather up the blossom dancing free.

Taking time to snuggle in
my dog's soft velvet fur.

Taking time to feel the beat of my cat's rhythmic purr.

Taking time to watch
with awe a spider
build her home.

Taking time to contemplate the journey as we roam.

Taking time to wonder at
the vast, astounding sky.

Taking time to gaze upon
a flock that passes by.

Taking time to find myself in eyes that are so kind.

Taking time to marvel at a snowflake soft and fine.

Taking time to imagine
the deep sounds of the sea.

Taking time to cherish you,
and also cherish me.

Can you remember which child
brought each keepsake?

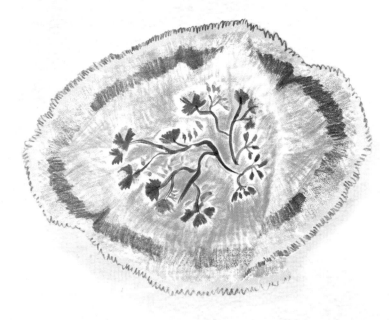